A
B♭
Your heart's in wide re - ceiv - ing, been too long bur - ied in the sand.
Dmaj7
E♭maj7
Some things re - quire be - liev - ing, this gift will fall right in your
F♯m7
Gm7
hand, just try to un - der -
Dmaj7
E♭maj7
stand. If you

A
B♭
long e - nough and you
Long e - nough, and you
Dmaj7
E♭maj7
don't give up. If you're
don't give up. If you're
A
B♭
strong e - nough and you
strong e - nough. Long e - nough, you've got to

Dmaj7
E♭maj7
don't give up. And you'll,
keep your faith, and you don't give up.
E
F
you'll be no har - bor to the sor -
D
E♭
row.
Dmaj7
E♭maj7
Spoken: *Just let it go.*

A
B♭
Dmaj7
E♭maj7
Na.
A
B♭
cresc. poco a poco
Dmaj7
E♭maj7
Na.

F♯m7
Gm7
Dmaj7
E♭maj7
A
B♭
Don't hang your head in sor - row, don't give up just__ be - fore__ you win._
Dmaj7
E♭maj7
__ Don't wait a-round for to - mor - row, o-pen up your arms_ and let it in.____
mf

A
B♭
This gift will last for - ev - er. This gift will nev - er let you down.
Dmaj7
E♭maj7
Some things are made from bet - ter stuff. This gift is read - y to be
F♯m7
Gm7
3
found, just you be - lieve it
Dmaj7
E♭maj7
now.

A
B♭
This gift will last for - ev - er. This gift will nev - er let you down.
Dmaj7
E♭maj7
Some things are made from bet - ter stuff. This gift is read - y to be found.
A
B♭
Your heart's in wide re - ceiv - ing, been too long bur-ied in the sand.
Dmaj7
E♭maj7
Some things re - quire be - liev - ing, these things just fall right in your

F♯m7
Gm7
hand, just try to un - der -
Dmaj7
E♭maj7
stand. If you
A
B♭
long e - nough and you
Strong e - nough, if you long e - nough, you've got to